Phineas F. Bresee:
Mr. Nazarene

PHINEAS F. BRESEE:

Mr. Nazarene

by
Emily Bushey Moore

Nazarene Publishing House
Kansas City, Missouri

First Printing, 1973

Printed in the
United States of America

ISBN: 0-8341-0157-2

Dedication

To my favorite elementary teacher, Mrs. William Esselstyn, known to me as Bessie Grose. She became my teacher when I was in the fourth grade and had a deep influence on my life. I shall never forget the sense of loss I felt the year she left our school to go to the mission field in Africa.

She and Dr. Esselstyn have now retired from missionary work and live in Michigan. I am indebted to them for reviewing this manuscript and giving most helpful constructive criticism.

—E. B. Moore

Contents

PHINEAS F. BRESEE
Founder of the Church of the Nazarene

1

"From the Time I Was Born"

It was winter in northern New York state, the last day of the year, 1838. Five miles from the little town of Franklin, smoke curled from the chimney of a log house. This cabin was the home of the Bresee (Bre-ZEE) family.

The surrounding farmland was covered by a deep blanket of snow. A cold wind was blowing, but it was warm and cozy inside. Burning logs crackled and sputtered in the fireplace.

Suddenly, a new sound rose above the gusty wind and sizzling fire. A baby's first cry filled the room. The little boy was the Bresees' second child. They gave him his father's first name, Phineas (FIN-ee-us).

From the very first, God's special care seemed to be over little Phineas. When he was about 15 months old, the family moved to another farm a few miles away. It was in the late winter of 1840. Heavy snow still lay on the ground.

Father loaded the family belongings on a big sled. He hitched up a team of oxen to pull the load. Then he helped Mother and Little Sister up on the high seat. Carefully he lifted

Baby Phineas to Mother's waiting arms, and then climbed up beside them.

With a jerk, the sled runners loosened from the frozen ground and soon were sliding along the snow-packed road. Things went smoothly until they came to the main road, which was more heavily travelled. There were other ox teams, sleighs, and horses. Father Bresee's team of oxen became frightened and took off into the bush. Fortunately the sled did not upset and no one was injured. Father jumped down and finally managed to get the oxen back on the road.

The new house was warmed by an iron heating stove in the center of the living room. In winter it kept Father busy cutting and splitting wood for the heater.

One winter evening, little two-year-old Phineas was ready for bed. He was jumping and running about in his red flannel nightgown when suddenly he tumbled against the hot stove. His screams brought Mother and Father rushing to his rescue. They quickly smothered the flames that leaped from his flannel gown, but his right leg was burned.

It was too far to go to town for help. Mother did the best thing she could think to do. She took thick cream from the top of the milk and spread it over Phineas' burned leg. The painful stinging stopped and his sobs quieted. Little Phineas fell asleep, not knowing how near he had come to tragedy.

A baby brother was born that year, but he lived to be only a year old. So Phineas had only an older sister to share his work and play.

Before he was four years old, Phineas' parents started him in school. One day he came home with his first book. "O Ma!" he called proudly, and opened his book to show her the pictures. "I have got clear over to the wolf." The fact is, Phineas never learned to read well. Only a few books were used at school and the class would read and reread the same things day after day.

Phineas had a very good memory and listened carefully to what was read. When it was his turn, he would look at the picture and, from memory, repeat word for word what the others had read.

"I could read first-rate," he said with a laugh, "because I knew the books by heart. But once in a while the teacher would have us read out of a newspaper, and I made bad work of it."

Phineas was not able to attend school regularly, but he was learning other things. Living in the foothills of the Catskill Mountains, he was surrounded by nature and beauty. He dearly loved to roam and play in the mountains, or to fish and swim in the Ouleout River, that flowed through the valley.

But this does not mean that he played all the time. Even when a very young boy he was taught to work on the farm. He drove the horses and oxen. He brought the cows from the pasture and helped milk them. He learned to work in the fields and do the plowing. He chopped and stacked kindling wood for the heater and the cookstove. He fed and cared for the farm animals and ran errands for his parents.

There really was not much time for either play or school. But his experience of hard work on the farm helped prepare him for a rugged life in the future.

There was something else he was learning—something very important. His parents taught him faith in God, faith in the Bible, and faith in the church. Every week the family attended the Methodist church in town. Little Phineas always went to Sunday school. He listened to the Bible stories and learned the memory verses.

In those days, it was often necessary for a preacher to pastor two or three churches. This was called a circuit of churches. The minister usually travelled by horse from one of his churches to another. He was called a circuit rider.

For these preachers, the Bresee home was always a welcome place to stop. There they might eat a meal or spend the night.

11

Phineas watched and listened to these ministers and secretly wanted to be like them. Even as a small child it was becoming clear to Phineas that he should someday be a minister.

A kind gentleman lived down by the main road. He was a large man and a leader in the community. One day he stopped to talk with little Phineas. In a friendly way, he laid his big hand on the boy's head and asked, "Now what are you going to do when you are a man?"

Phineas was too shy and embarrassed to say anything.

"Let me see." The big man thought a moment. "Maybe you will be a farmer like your father, or maybe a doctor, or a teacher?"

Still the small boy made no answer.

"Oh, I know," the kind man decided, "you will be a minister, won't you?"

Phineas blushed, but his face must have lit up in response. The big man smiled, "Oh, yes, that is it. That is the noblest calling of all."

Phineas wondered why everyone didn't know what had been on his mind all along.

2

"I Will Go"

Phineas was 12 years old and very excited. His father had traded their farm in on a much more valuable place. The new property was one of the most beautiful in all that section of the country.

Eagerly young Phineas inspected the many fine buildings. He could hardly believe what he saw. Proudly he described the farm to his curious friends. "It is almost like a little village," he told them. But Phineas soon found that such a farm meant more work.

His parents wanted him to continue going to school. They sent him to two academies. He went to Oneonta for a couple of years, and then to Franklin. But the strain of studying and doing farm work at the same time was too much, even for a strong, healthy boy. He had to quit school.

Yet something very wonderful had happened to him at the Franklin Academy. A deep desire to learn had come over him. Although he no longer attended school, he spent all his spare time studying.

The subjects he enjoyed most were the very old languages

of Latin and Greek. Learning Greek was especially useful in helping young Phineas to understand and love the Scriptures.

The town of Franklin was a good community with friendly, warmhearted folks. Besides its excellent academy, there was a small library in the town. It had books to loan to those, like Phineas, who wanted to read and learn at home. In the center of town, towering above the other buildings, was the white church steeple pointing to the sky.

Phineas looked forward to the weekly shopping trips to town. The family would go to the general store, which had everything one needed in those days. While Mother would shop for cloth or groceries, Father would study the tools and equipment on sale. Perhaps there was a new shipment of horse collars, guns, or axes.

In the summer, Father would talk with the other farmers as they waited around outside the store. In the winter, they would gather inside. Seated around the warm, potbellied stove, they exchanged bits of news or discussed farm problems.

Phineas tried to be grownup and join them. But he found it hard to keep his eyes from wandering to the shelf of toys or to the big jars of candy.

If one of his father's horses needed to be shod, Phineas went along to the blacksmith's shop. He watched the blacksmith working at his blazing forge. He saw how he pumped the air bellows to keep the fire glowing. With long tongs the smith held the horseshoe in the hot fire until it glowed red. Then he carefully hammered it into shape on the anvil, so it would fit the horse's hoof.

When the shoe was ready, Phineas helped hold the horse steady while the shoe was nailed to the horse's hoof. He knew this did not hurt the horse, but protected its hoof. Phineas was kind to horses and learned how to handle them well.

The town of Franklin was very special to Phineas. He dearly

loved it. In fact, when he began to think that he would like to have a middle name, he asked his parents if he might use the name of Franklin. So, after that, he went by the name of Phineas Franklin Bresee.

But Franklin was not to be his hometown much longer. When he was about 16 years old, his father sold the big farm and bought a half interest in a store in nearby West Davenport. In the contract, it was agreed that young Phineas was to serve as a clerk in the store for five years.

One day, when he was working at the store, his new pastor stopped to see him. The minister and his helper were holding meetings at the church every night. Such continued services were called "protracted meetings."

Phineas was not busy with customers, so the pastor invited him to the meetings and talked to him about the things of God. He urged him to seek salvation. "You should ask God to forgive your sins, Phineas."

Phineas knew the pastor was right. A feeling of uneasiness swept over him. He realized he was a sinner. His heart was heavy with guilt. He decided he would go to the meetings and seek salvation.

After the preaching that night, Phineas went forward to kneel at the altar rail and pray. But somehow he did not feel relief from his guilt.

Sunday afternoon there was a special testimony meeting called a "class meeting." During the meeting Phineas confessed that he did not feel that his sins were forgiven. So the group all kneeled down to pray for him again. Soon a wonderful peace came over him. No one had to tell him his sins were forgiven. He knew God had saved him from his sins.

Without waiting, he began to do Christian work. He would hold prayer meetings and talk to people about being saved.

In a few months, the pastor gave Phineas an "exhorter's"

15

license. (This is like a beginner's license to preach.) Perhaps the pastor thought this would encourage the young teen-ager to try even harder. But being very bashful, Phineas was almost ready to give up. Though church groups were expecting him to come and have part in a service, he sometimes did not show up. He was afraid. He realized he was not prepared.

He still felt God wanted him to preach, but he was troubled. How could a bashful person like him ever become a preacher? Also, he was still under contract to work at the store for three more years.

Earnestly he talked to God about his problem. "Well, Lord," he prayed, "I am tied up here. But if You will open the way, I will go anywhere You can use me."

In just a few weeks, like an answer to his prayer, his father sold his partnership in the store. Phineas was free from the work contract.

The family began making plans to move out West to the plains of Iowa. Phineas' friends learned of this. They insisted that he should preach before he left.

An appointment was made for him to preach one Sunday afternoon at a little church not far from Davenport. "I went down there with the junior preacher," he recalled, "and preached, or tried to."

Phineas read a Bible verse from Psalms 124:7 about a bird being escaped from a trap. Then he bravely began to preach. He went all the way from creation, through the Old Testament to the coming of Jesus, then on down to his own conversion and on to the future judgment. He said many years afterward, "Although I put everything I knew in it, it was only about 20 minutes long. I wondered what in the world a fellow would ever preach about at another sermon."

When the family moved to Iowa he still had only that one sermon.

16

3

A Minister, Ordained of God

For a teen-age boy in 1856, moving from New York to Iowa was a big change. Phineas found that much of Iowa was still a wilderness of unsettled prairie. Very little religious work was being done. Services were sometimes held in schoolhouses or homes. Church buildings were very scarce.

There was a great need for someone to hold meetings. Phineas remembered his promise to God to preach if He would open the way. When people learned that he had a license to "exhort," they pressed him into Christian service.

An older minister recommended him for a district preacher's license in the Methodist conference. At once he was appointed to help a pastor who had a circuit of several preaching points.

The area assigned them was undeveloped. It took four weeks for the two of them to get to all their services. Phineas was glad he had learned to handle a horse well, for there was no other means of transportation.

There were no church buildings on the circuit. The people used schoolhouses and homes for their services. Phineas worked hard getting new people together and starting Sunday schools and preaching points.

He especially remembered one log cabin where they held meetings. It was the home of a man named Jones. They called it, "Davy Jones's Locker." It did not look as if there were any other houses for miles. But hidden away in the valleys were other pioneer cottages. The people would come in their wagons to take part in the services.

While Phineas or the other minister tried to preach, the odors from the kitchen became distracting. Mrs. Jones kept busy during the service preparing dinner for all of them. But in spite of the simple setting, the meetings were a blessing to those isolated people. Many found help from the Lord.

Phineas began to do more of the preaching. He was a sincere, ambitious young man. The rugged life and the hard work did not discourage him. The older minister was pleased and had great hopes for him as a preacher.

Phineas began holding protracted meetings. Every night for several weeks he would preach at some church on the circuit. At two of these preaching points the meetings became great revivals and many were converted.

Before his twentieth birthday, he was sent to pastor a Methodist church in a town called Pella. The work there was difficult. Most of the people were from Holland and did not speak much English. Another church which had a strong influence in the community, was already there. It even had a college in connection with it.

Phineas was paid very little money. The members of the church gave him food, but that did not help him when he needed to buy clothes. God helped him, however, and supplied his needs.

Often he felt lonely during those two years at Pella, so he began to write letters to a friend back in New York. His name was Nat Hibbard. They had worked together in the store at

Davenport. Phineas had often visited the Hibbard farm. Nat's father was the Sunday school superintendent and was a hardworking church layman.

Nat had a sister named Maria, a fine Christian girl. Phineas liked her quite well and once in a while he wrote to her, too.

Reading Nat's letters made him think more and more about Maria. Finally he made up his mind that he would ask her if she would marry him. He began writing serious letters to her about becoming his wife.

At the close of his two years at Pella, in 1860, Phineas made a trip back to New York. There he and Maria were married.

Mrs. Hibbard had been very worried about the sacrifices her daughter would have to make if she moved away out to Iowa. She warned her that she would not have many of the things she needed. But this did not bother Maria. Gladly she went with Phineas. She felt it would please God for her to help Phineas win people to Christ.

Two or three weeks after their marriage, the young couple went back to Iowa. Phineas took his bride to his parents' home for a short visit. Then they went to the district church conference. At the conference, Phineas was appointed to the church at Grinnell.

Grinnell was a circuit of five preaching points. Every Sunday, Phineas would preach three times. In the morning he would preach at one church. Then he would get on his horse or wagon and go to preach in the afternoon at another place. In the evening he would travel to still another church. The next Sunday he would go to the churches he missed the previous week.

Mrs. Hibbard's fears for her daughter were right. The year was one of great hardship.

"We lived largely on faith," Phineas said. "You would hardly believe that one sack of flour, with a few pounds of buckwheat to make pancakes, did us that year."

At this time the nation was very much upset over the problem of owning slaves. In the southern states there were many Negro slaves working on the plantations. Most of the owners loved their slaves and took good care of them, but others treated them cruelly.

In the North there were very few slaves. The northern people, for the most part, felt it was wrong to "own" black men. They said it was wicked to buy and sell them like farm livestock. Phineas Bresee felt very strongly that it was sinful. He began preaching against slavery.

When the northerners got laws passed to do away with slavery, the southern states decided they would not be part of the United States anymore. They tried to become a separate nation. Abraham Lincoln, who was president at the time, felt strongly that the United States must be kept as one nation at any cost.

But a horrible war broke out between the South and the North. It was called the Civil War. Many young men went to battle. Phineas' friend, Nat, was one of them. He was not killed, but he came back in such poor health that he died soon after his sister married Phineas.

Phineas believed so firmly in the Union that he made it a practice to drape his pulpit with the American flag. He loved his native land and in his prayers at his services often prayed that God would bless this nation and its leaders.

One of the churches on his Grinnell circuit was in an area made up mainly of people who had come from the South. They disliked young Bresee's firm stand for the Union. His preaching against slavery offended them.

They felt the South was right and began to be very unfriendly toward their pastor. Phineas realized their dislike for him, so at the end of the church year he asked to be sent to a different appointment.

That year at the conference, Phineas knelt for a special

honor. The bishop, who was the head minister over the district, laid his hands on the young pastor's head. He prayed for him and declared him an ordained elder. This meant that Rev. Phineas F. Bresee was now a minister in full standing in the Methodist church.

To Mr. Bresee, this ceremony meant more than just a church giving him credential papers that said he was a preacher. He knew he had been chosen and ordained of God to be a minister of the gospel. He determined to be the best minister possible for both God and the church.

4

Tested and Tried

Being ordained didn't mean that Phineas Bresee would be given a better church. In fact he found himself appointed to the poorest circuit of churches in the conference.

The circuit was out on the prairie, with no church buildings and no parsonage. There were six preaching places, most of them in small, one-room schoolhouses. It was called the Galesburg circuit. Galesburg was the name of a little settlement of four or five houses where only about 20 people lived.

The young preacher felt deeply hurt about the appointment, but he told no one. Instead, he made up his mind that with God's help he would succeed in spite of the big problems.

While he had been away at the conference, their first child had been born. They named the baby boy Ernest. How could they move with such a small baby? Where would they live? How would they manage to pay the bills they owed? There was certainly no money at Galesburg. How would they buy the things they needed?

Before moving, Mr. Bresee sold his good horse and bought a

poorer one, so he could pay his bills. Then he took his little family to Galesburg.

At first the only place he could find to live in was a two-room "apartment" in a house. To get to their rooms they had to go through the owner's living room. Fortunately they were soon able to find a better place.

Instead of paying their minister money, the people brought him produce that they raised on their farms—mostly wheat and hogs. But again God saw that they had the things they needed.

One day a Methodist preacher stopped at the Bresee home. He had been forced to leave Missouri because he preached against slavery. Mr. Bresee, in his kind way, took the man in and tried to help him.

This meant added expense for the family, but Mr. Bresee was determined not to go into debt again. So together the two preachers rented some prairie land and raised wheat. Mr. Bresee bought a pair of mules and broke them in for work. It took a while to get them tamed but when that was done, Mr. Bresee said those mules "made the gayest little team that I ever saw. They were just two rabbits in their get-up and travel. If I wanted to go five or six miles, they would run with all their might."

Mr. Bresee worked very hard that year. He visited at every farmhouse, invited people to church, preached with all his heart, and built up the work.

The very first week he was there, he announced a protracted meeting to start in just two weeks. It began in October with services every night, and lasted until spring. The revival spirit spread to all six preaching places. People came for miles to his meetings and filled the schoolhouses where he preached.

After preaching, he would give an invitation for sinners to come to pray at the altar. If they did not come, he would go out among the people and speak to them about seeking the Lord. As soon as he persuaded one to kneel right where he was, he would

23

call the members to gather around and pray for the seeker. He tried everything to win souls to the Lord. He felt he had nothing to lose and was determined to succeed.

"That charge," he said, "did me more good than any I ever had." It taught him that it took earnestness and intensity to be successful in doing God's work.

When conference time came around again, Mr. Bresee was assigned to a church in Des Moines. When he arrived he found that the church had big debts. But the young pastor was able to get the church on a good financial footing. With his revival methods, the church made very good progress spiritually as well.

During their stay in Des Moines, the Bresees' second child was born. The baby girl was beautiful but she was not strong and was sick much of the time. They named her Lily and took very tender care of her.

At the close of their second year there, the Bresees made a trip back to New York. They took their two small children. But while they were in New York, the baby became very sick, and they were not able to get back in time for the yearly conference.

A surprise was waiting for Mr. Bresee when he reached Iowa. Instead of being assigned to pastor a church, he learned that he had been appointed to be a presiding elder. He was to have charge over a large group of churches. This meant that he must travel much of the time, visiting pastors and preaching at their churches.

There were no fast ways to travel in those days: no cars, busses, or airplanes. Usually Mr. Bresee rode in a buggy pulled by a pair of ponies. This was slow, but he made good use of his time. While the animals would jog along, Mr. Bresee would pray, study, and read.

He read many good books. Some of them were hard to understand, but he would study them carefully. Year by year he added new books to his growing library. He was becoming a well-educated gentleman.

On his longer trips, which took several weeks, he liked to take Mrs. Bresee and the children with him. On one of these trips, little Lily, just 15 months old, became sick and died. This was heartbreaking but God helped the parents trust it all to His care. Bravely they returned to Des Moines for the funeral.

Being presiding elder was difficult. Travel was tiring. Meals were irregular and not always the best. Mr. Bresee had to sleep in many different homes and sometimes in uncomfortable beds. The schedule of services was almost beyond his strength at times.

Often he held all-day conference meetings. He was expected to lead the early morning prayer meeting. Then at 9 a.m. he conducted a testimony sharing time, called a "love feast," and then preached at 10:30. This was followed by a lengthy Communion service until 2:30 in the afternoon. When dinner was finally ready, he would be almost too weak to eat. Still later in the evening, an out-of-door meeting was held in a grove of trees, where he had to preach again.

During these days Mr. Bresee faced deep testing of his own faith. He knew God had forgiven him of his sins when he was a young teen-ager. He was also doing his best to work for the Lord. Yet he was troubled within sometimes by feelings of anger, pride, and ambition. This bothered him and caused him to doubt God. He knew he needed a deeper experience with God that would clear out this inner problem. He asked God to show him what he should do to get rid of his doubts and questions.

5

"Nobody Got Sanctified but Myself"

The biting snow blew fiercely across the prairies. The thermometer in Chariton, Ia., where the Bresees were now pastoring, dropped to 20 degrees below zero. At the back of the sanctuary the big heating stove glowed red. Near it huddled the few brave folks who had come to church on that stormy night in 1867.

Mr. Bresee preached the best he could and then, as usual, gave an invitation for those who needed to be saved to come to the altar. No one came. Then he had a strong feeling that he should go himself. It seemed to him that he could not continue to preach when he was so filled with doubts.

He did not know just how he should pray, but he poured out his heart to God asking for His help. The Lord did answer his prayer and the Holy Spirit came in to purify his heart. He said he felt as if heaven was poured out on him. His tendencies to worldliness, anger, and pride were taken away and also the doubt.

In remembering the meeting at Chariton, Mr. Bresee said, "Nobody got sanctified but myself, and I did not know anything about [the teaching]."

He had not heard any preaching about such a "second blessing." Yet when he yielded himself completely to God that night, he found the experience. After that, entire sanctification (as it was called) was to be an all-important doctrine to preach to the people.

Although Mr. Bresee now had victory in his own Christian life, pastoring in Chariton was just as difficult as before. There was no parsonage and for a year the Bresees had to live in part of a house, where they had only one room and a tiny kitchen.

The room had to be their bedroom, study, dining room, and parlor. They even had to make their beds on the floor. A young woman who lived in the next room taught piano lessons. At times the sound became unbearable to the Bresees.

The second year they found a cottage with four rooms. This gave them the space they needed but still did not solve the problem of getting food to eat. They often were without butter, meat, and other necessary things.

Shortly before they left Chariton, their daughter Bertha was born. This meant added needs for the family, but God cared for them. Through all the hardships, the Bresees had a new and deeper trust in God.

At conference time Phineas Bresee was sent back to the church in Des Moines where he had pastored once before. The people there noticed that his preaching was different. Mr. Bresee had begun preaching about being sanctified. He told the people there was an additional experience that a Christian could find after being converted. They could be filled with the Holy Spirit. He did not know very well how to explain this experience to them, but he knew what had happened to him and he wanted others to enjoy this closer walk with God.

Several Christians were sanctified in those meetings. The change in their lives was easy to see. With such results, Mr. Bresee's faith became much stronger.

His next appointment was to Council Bluffs. This was a difficult Mormon center, but God helped him increase his congregation. He saw several persons sanctified during his pastorate there.

In 1871, Mr. Bresee was elected as a delegate from his district to go to the General Conference of the Methodist church. It was held that year in Brooklyn, N.Y. Delegates from all over the world were there. Mr. Bresee was probably the youngest member of the General Conference. But in spite of this, in a quiet way, he helped make decisions for the denomination.

During the three years the Bresees were at Council Bluffs, two more sons were born into the family, Paul and Melvin. The Bresee house was indeed a busy home.

From there, Mr. Bresee went to pastor at Red Oak. Grandpa and Grandma Bresee came to live with their son. The church gave their pastor a good salary and a fine parsonage. After many years of need, the family now lived in comparative comfort. Their youngest child, Susan, was born there.

The church at Red Oak had a marvelous revival while Mr. Bresee was their pastor. The rich and the poor, the prominent people and the social outcasts came and were converted. These went out to bring their families and friends to find God. Mr. Bresee said it was the greatest revival in which he had ever had a part.

There were more converts than there were seating spaces in the church building. Something had to be done. So after much persuading, planning, praying, and preaching, a beautiful new church and parsonage were built. Still today in the Methodist church at Red Oak, there hangs a picture of Rev. Phineas F. Bresee.

6

To California

Three other church assignments followed in Iowa: Clarinda, Creston, and then back to Council Bluffs. At each church Mr. Bresee was able to have a revival and increase the size of the membership. But there was a rule then that no pastor could stay at one place for over three years.

The Bresees now had six living children, Lily having died several years before. They were Ernest, Phineas W., Bertha, Paul, Melvin, and Susan. Mr. Bresee's parents lived with them too. This was a large family to feed and care for. The salary from pastoring never seemed to be quite enough. Sometimes Mr. Bresee was tempted to look for other ways to add to the family income.

But God had a way to meet the need. When a prosperous relative died, a large sum of money came to him as an inheritance. No longer did the Bresee family lack for food and clothes. They began to live more comfortably. Mr. Bresee tried to find wise ways to use his money, so that it would increase. He turned for advice to one of his friends, Rev. Joseph Knott.

Mr. Knott had had to give up preaching because of a lung

illness. He had started a business with a bookstore and the printing of a Christian paper. He asked Mr. Bresee to become editor of his magazine.

This project did not last long, for a fire destroyed the building they were using. Their stock of books and paper was completely ruined.

Mr. Knott had other property and began to look for places to invest his money. He found out about a silver mine in Mexico and persuaded Mr. Bresee and others to put their money with some of his to buy it.

Soon after work was started in the old mine, there was a big explosion. An underground river poured into the tunnels. The workmen barely escaped. The expensive machinery and tools had to be left behind. The venture failed and the investors lost all their money.

Mr. Bresee sold what he could, to pay his bills. But he found he was once again without any money or property. The family began to feel the pinch of poverty. After this disaster Mr. Bresee made a vow that he would never again attempt to make money, but would give the remainder of his life completely to the preaching of the Word of God.

He felt too ashamed and embarrassed to stay in Iowa. Here the people thought he was successful and prosperous. He decided that the best thing to do was to go to a distant part of the country and start over. Friends had told him about the new settlements in California. This might be a good place to go. He prayed about the matter and felt God would be pleased. But how could he afford to move his large family all the way to California?

Mr. Bresee was not the only one who was embarrassed by his money failure. Since Mr. Knott had asked him to invest in the doomed silver mine, he felt responsible. He gave his friend Bresee a gift of $1,000 to make his trip.

The Bresee family had a friend in Nebraska who was an

official in the railroad company. They wrote to him about their proposed trip. The man had an empty railroad car sent to them in Council Bluffs.

They began fitting it with furniture and curtains, so they could live and travel in it as well as carry all their goods with them. At last all was ready. Their car was coupled to a string of other cars. The excited family, with Grandma and Grandpa and a few friends, climbed into their traveling home. The engine whistled and slowly the train began moving down the track. The travellers waved good-by and then settled down for their long, jiggly trip west.

Some days the car was fastened to a passenger train and they made good progress. Other days they found themselves pulled by a slow freight train that stopped at every little crossroads station. When their car was put off on a sidetrack to wait, the family enjoyed getting out and walking about the nearby town.

Back in 1883, much of the West was still unsettled. From their window, the family saw the rolling prairie land, the level plains, the rugged mountains, the rivers and forests. At times they caught sight of Indians or of wild animals. There were buffalo, antelope, and jack rabbits. The excited children held their breath as the train groaned up steep mountain grades, crossed over high bridge tressels, or was swallowed up in dark tunnels.

But after eight days of travel, they finally reached Los Angeles. They had sent word to a friend to tell of their coming. A furnished house was rented and waiting for them.

They arrived on Saturday afternoon, but Mrs. Bresee managed to have all their Sunday clothes ready by that night. They would not think of missing church. They had decided to attend First Methodist Church, which at that time had 385 members.

Los Angeles was just a small city then. But it took the Bresee family longer to get to church than they expected. Coming

31

in a little late, Mr. Bresee was surprised to be ushered right up to the pulpit. The pastor introduced him and asked him to preach.

There was no time to prepare a new sermon. Mr. Bresee prayed a quick, silent prayer for God's help and arose to speak. He was not a tall man, but his appearance held every eye. His broad shoulders marked him as a man of strength. He was neatly dressed in the long, black coat usually worn by ministers in that day.

But it was his rather round face that drew the most attention. Behind a heavy, dark beard were hidden a firm chin and set lips. His black hair framed his balding forehead. Dark, expressive eyes looked out tenderly on the audience.

When he spoke, his rich voice carried to the farthest corners of the big auditorium. His words were well chosen. People realized that he felt very deeply what he said. They saw he was indeed a strong man, not just in his body, but in his spiritual life. Indeed, he was a leader of men. Yet they sensed that he was humble in spirit and was more concerned about helping them than about making a good impression. He wanted everyone to know the joy of full salvation.

Two weeks later, at the California conference, Mr. Bresee was appointed to be the pastor of that very church. For three years he pastored there and the membership of the church almost doubled. Mr. Bresee, at 45 years of age, was being well accepted in the Methodist conference in California. Surely God would use him in a mighty way in the denomination he loved so dearly.

7

A Fresh Anointing

In the Los Angeles First Church, Mr. Bresee found a small group of active holiness people. Quietly they prayed and worked to see their Christian friends sanctified.

In his own life, Mr. Bresee had received this baptism of the Holy Spirit back in Iowa. But he had found it without knowing very much about the doctrine. Since that time, he had faithfully preached holiness, trying to lead others into the experience. But he began to feel that he should be doing more than he was. He should be preaching more definitely on the subject.

In 1884, two holiness evangelists came to California. They held a series of meetings in his church. He liked their spirit and did what he could to make the services a success. Several were sanctified.

God began to give Mr. Bresee a deeper understanding of holiness. He had a growing desire for a fresh anointing or blessing in his own life. For weeks he prayed to God for greater spiritual power in his preaching.

God had a special holiness ministry to which He was calling

Mr. Bresee. As if to prepare him for this work, God gave to him a very unusual heavenly blessing. It was so personal and sacred that he told only a few close friends. From that time on, he had a new sense of power in his ministry.

Holiness became the one important message of his preaching. To be sanctified was no longer to him a sort of dessert to be taken or left. This baptism of the Holy Spirit was a necessary part of salvation. He emphasized the Bible verse, "Holiness, without which no man shall see the Lord" (Hebrews 21:14b).

Mr. Bresee enjoyed his pastorate in Los Angeles First Church. He saw the work grow and prosper. He was loved by the people. A wonderful spirit of revival continued the three years he was there.

He did not want to leave, but at conference time he was sent to the nearby city of Pasadena. Pasadena was then a new town. Only a few years before, it had been a sheep ranch. Now it was growing very fast. New buildings and homes were going up constantly.

At this time a new Methodist church was being built. Soon it was finished and dedicated, but in a short time the crowds were too large for the building. Mr. Bresee persuaded the church to build a big tabernacle beside it that would seat 2,000 people. The first building was used for Sunday school and other meetings.

Just before church time, Mr. Bresee would hold street meetings on a main corner in town. His people would sing and testify and crowds would gather to listen. He would invite them to church, then lead a march to the church building. A large number would follow. A great revival began with many new converts being won.

About this time a great drive was started in the city to do away with the sale of alcoholic drinks. The battle was a hot one. Mr. Bresee became the leader. Boldly he blasted the evil forces with his preaching.

34

The liquor leaders became intensely angry. They made a dummy to look like Mr. Bresee and burned it in a public street. Instead of hindering the temperance work, this made good publicity for Mr. Bresee. Many more came to hear him preach and got behind the movement.

After one fiery sermon against strong drink, he received a threatening letter. It warned Mr. Bresee that if he did not stop preaching against the liquor business he "would get *that*." Underneath was a drawing of a pistol.

Mr. Bresee was a humble, modest man. Yet he feared no one but God. He ignored threats and ridicule about him or his work. It was mainly through the efforts of this brave preacher that Pasadena remained a "dry" city.

When the dry forces won, the liquor dealers were furious. A mob stormed the Methodist parsonage, threatening the pastor's life. But God protected the Bresees.

Mr. Bresee made other efforts as a Christian leader to help with community problems. In Pasadena there were many Chinese who had been brought to California to work. In loving concern, Mr. Bresee founded a thriving mission to help them. He also tried to get the Methodist conference to begin other such missions.

About this time the possible term of a Methodist pastor's stay was lengthened from three years to five. Mr. Bresee remained the fourth year at Pasadena. During those four years he took 1,000 members into the church.

He continued his preaching on holiness and urged his converts to seek the experience. But opposition began to develop. A few important, wealthy members did not want him to return a fifth year. They wanted a "fashionable" church. They did not like Mr. Bresee's preaching on living a holy life. He had never met such objection to his preaching before and he was troubled.

Rather than stir up further trouble, he resigned and went to a smaller church. The following year he was appointed presiding elder over the Los Angeles District. Much of that year he spent holding revivals and tent meetings throughout the district.

Mr. Bresee wanted a spirit of holiness revival to continue in the Methodist church. He loved his church deeply. At conference the next year, he proposed a day of prayer and fasting for the spiritual life of the church.

But the bishop in charge of the conference was not a holiness man. He removed Mr. Bresee from the position of presiding elder. He sent him to a small church which was deeply in debt. After a year, Mr. Bresee felt the work there was useless. He told the board he could not return and made suggestions for changing the situation there.

Mr. Bresee was then sent to an even smaller church in Los Angles. He worked there for a year with some success. But a new field of service was calling to him. Mission work for the poor and neglected of the city drew his attention.

8

"Out Under the Stars"

"Dr. Bresee!" A new title had been added to the name of Phineas F. Bresee. The honorary degree of doctor of divinity had been given to him by the University of Southern California.

Being a humble man, he felt unworthy, for he had very little school education. But the title was fitting to his ability. Soon everyone was calling him "Dr. Bresee."

In 1883, when he had come to California, he was chosen to be a member of the board of directors of the University of Southern California. He continued in that office until 1895.

At the university, he worked closely with a good man of great influence, Dr. J. P. Widney. It may have been he who recommended Dr. Bresee for the honorary degree. The two men became close friends.

Dr. Widney was one of the best known physicians in California. He was an educator, speaker, reformer, and writer. Indeed, he was a very talented and prosperous man.

In 1892, Dr. Widney became president of the university.

The school was near ruin because of its debts. Together with Dr. Bresee, he set out to rescue it from failure. He made Dr. Bresee chairman of a new governing board. Within two years their plans had saved the school from closing.

With the school in good financial standing again, he and Dr. Bresee turned to a new project. For many years Dr. Bresee had felt a growing concern to reach poor people for Jesus. He saw that the churches were doing nothing to win these needy people. The poor did not feel welcome to worship in the churches. He was so moved by the need that he was willing to give the rest of his life to their cause.

About this time a group of independent holiness people in Los Angeles received a large sum of money for just such a mission project. They invited Dr. Widney and Dr. Bresee into their fellowship to help launch the work.

At first Dr. Bresee was not sure what he should do. But as he prayed about the matter he became persuaded to help. He agreed to organize the mission. He located property and helped them start a building. The group decided to name the work Peniel Mission.

Because of the nature of the original gift for the mission, it could not be organized under the direction of any one church or denomination. Yet Dr. Bresee felt certain that the Methodist conference would not object to his working there.

At conference time he wrote out a request to the bishop. He asked that instead of pastoring a church, he be given a special assignment to serve at the Peniel Mission. If this were not possible, he asked that he be granted the same standing as a retired minister.

Dr. Bresee was now 55 years of age. He had served the Methodist church for over 37 years. According to their rules, he was entitled to such a "supernumerary relation."

Either the bishop or other leading members of the conference refused his request. They felt that his working in such a mission would hurt the image of their church.

Dr. Bresee was loved and highly respected by most people of the conference. He had built up every church he had pastored by winning hundreds of people to Christ and the Methodist church. Yet for some time certain church leaders had opposed his holiness preaching. They did not like his evangelistic ways either.

Through the years the bishops had tried to make him change his emphasis. They had placed him in small and difficult churches. But Dr. Bresee had not complained. He loved the Methodist church and believed in her teachings. He had no thought of leaving it. His deep concern was to keep a revival spirit on the church. He had a special desire to emphasize the doctrine of entire sanctification as a second work of grace. This had been the teaching of the founder of Methodism, John Wesley.

John Wesley taught that this "second blessing" was an experience which came when the Christian completely turned his life over to God. It was a baptism or infilling of the Holy Spirit. The sinful nature was cleansed and the heart was filled with perfect love toward God and one's fellowman. This sanctified Christian was still human and imperfect in his thoughts and actions, yet his desires and purposes were right before God.

Dr. Bresee now found himself in an awkward position. He had already begun work at the Peniel Mission. He had felt it was God's leading. Now, because of the action of the conference, he had a most difficult choice to make. If he continued in the mission work, he could no longer be a minister of the church he had loved and served so faithfully. What should he do?

He spent a long night in earnest prayer. He made his decision. The following day he asked that his name be taken from the Methodist Conference roll of elders.

"I was now out of the Conference," he related sadly. "I had

39

been a member from the time of my boyhood. My heart was full of almost unbearable sadness."

The work of Peniel Mission continued to grow. Dr. Bresee busied himself writing up a statement of their beliefs and purposes. He influenced many friends to give their time and money to help with the work. The new building was soon completed. A great crowd attended the dedication service.

During the summer that followed, Dr. Bresee traveled to the East to hold several camp meetings. He visited city missions to find ideas for operating the work in Los Angeles.

The last meeting of the summer was in Nebraska. He was eager to return to his family and to the work in Peniel Mission. But during this camp meeting a shocking letter arrived from his co-workers in Peniel. It gave no reasons, but simply stated that his services were no longer needed at the mission.

His hopes were shattered, but he did not falter or lose his faith. God helped him to continue with the camp meeting as though nothing had happened. But the future looked dark before him.

What could he do? He was now without a church denomination. He was without a place to preach. He was without credentials as a minister. He was without income.

Bravely he returned to California. He discovered that his friends had not forsaken him. Together with Dr. Widney they urged him to start a new church. It would be a mission church to reach the poor where he could preach holiness all he wished. They promised to stand behind him.

Earnestly he prayed for God's guidance. In a few days his decision was reached. With God's help he would dare to go "out under the stars" and organize a holiness work.

9

The Glory Barn

It was October 6, 1895. A large crowd filled a rented hall on South Main Street in Los Angeles. The room rang with praises to God. Dr. Bresee arose to preach. He took his text from Jeremiah, "Ask for the old paths, where is the good way, and walk therein, and ye shall find rest for your souls." It was an inspiring sermon.

"Reformers have not led men into new paths, but back to old truths. Luther and Wesley preached no new truth or doctrine. . . . The modern method of educating men into salvation . . . is insufficient. . . . Conversion and sanctification must be experienced," he said.

The next Sunday another meeting was held. An announcement was made that the following Sunday a new church would be organized. Dr. Widney suggested that it be called THE CHURCH OF THE NAZARENE, in honor of the Christ, the lowly Nazarene.

On October 20, 1895, a total of 82 men and women came forward from the audience and pledged themselves to the new work. The list of charter members was kept open for a few days. When completed it reached a total of 135. Several of the families who joined had strong church backgrounds. But many of these

41

first members were recent converts from the poorer sections of the city.

The owners of the building were upset. These worshipers were not very quiet. Their prayers were too strong. Their singing could be heard all over the neighborhood. Their shouts of praise seemed entirely too loud. The neighbors were complaining. Before a month ended, Dr. Bresee and his group were asked to move.

They moved up the street to an old hall that was soon to be torn down. There they worshiped for four months.

It bothered Dr. Bresee to see huge sums being spent to build fancy churches. One day as Dr. Bresee drove his horse and buggy down Grand Avenue he prayed that God would send some money for a Church of the Nazarene.

The Lord spoke to his troubled heart. "I have given myself to you." This encouraged him and with joy he declared that out under the stars was a good enough place for him. After all, Christ had nowhere to lay His head, yet He gave himself.

Soon a lot was leased and money borrowed to buy lumber for a plain board tabernacle. Since it was to be a simple, wood building, there would be no cornerstone to lay. But Dr. Bresee wanted all his members to have a part in a building ceremony, so he decided to have a "corner nail" ritual.

A big spike was started into a corner beam. Each member of the church, in his turn, took the hammer and struck the nail. It was well driven into the wall. People sang, shouted, and praised God during the service.

After the tabernacle was completed, the crowds came and continued to grow. Soon it was too small. Dr. Bresee was a man of vision. One Sunday he preached to his people about the need for a bigger building and announced that a special offering would be taken for this purpose.

On the appointed day, a large table was placed over the

altar. Then the people marched past and laid their money on the table. Many of them shouted and praised God as they did so. There was enough to make the needed expansion.

The enlarged building was little more than a great shed, but there the group worshiped for seven years. In describing it, Dr. Bresee said:

> This board tabernacle to us is far more beautiful than the most costly marble temple that was ever reared. Here we have seen the Lord. Here in a marvelous way He has been pleased to manifest His power to save. Here He has revealed His glory.

The tabernacle came to be called "The Glory Barn." Its fame began to spread. Tourists, coming to the city, asked to see it. Many visitors found the experience of holiness there and returned to their hometowns to testify to this second blessing. The story of the Church of the Nazarene began to spread across the country.

Though the building was rough and plain, the pastors and leading laymen were highly respected citizens. The result was that both rich and poor, high and low felt welcome there and very much at home.

Dr. Bresee and Dr. Widney worked as co-pastors and superintendents. They planned a democratic organization and gave as many people as possible something to do. Dr. Bresee busied his people with helping the needy. He had groups visiting jails and hospitals. Others held street meetings and prayer services in the homes.

He would urge people never to let others know what they gave in the offering. "This is a church of poor people," he would say. "I want the poorest to give without being embarrassed and the richest to come without being begged."

The church leaders felt that the Holy Spirit should guide the lives of its converts. So they made only a few general rules for

43

conduct. They kept the teaching of perfect love, or holiness, as the center of their creed.

Dr. Bresee believed people should enjoy their religion. Perhaps one feature that made this church different was its joyful, free spirit of worship.

Sundays at the old tabernacle were a kind of holy holiday. Families drove in with their horses and buggies, walked, or rode the city streetcars. They brought a basket dinner and prepared to spend the day. After the morning service, everyone ate together. In the afternoon they joined in a praise service or visited families in the community. Almost everyone stayed for the evening meeting.

Dr. Bresee seemed to be able to fit into every occasion. When he was in the pulpit, people loved to listen to him preach. But they also liked to see him dedicate a baby, perform a wedding, or conduct a Communion service. He seemed to know how to do everything just right. He thought about everyone there and carefully watched over every part of the service.

He always wanted his people to feel at home. He liked to have them take part in the services, to praise the Lord, and to testify. He was building a church for ordinary people.

He could not sing well and had difficulty keeping on tune. But he loved both the old hymns and the new gospel songs. He got into the habit of clapping his hands while the people sang. Soon the audience did the same. It became almost a custom to clap through the chorus of nearly every song.

When he stood to preach, everyone gave him attention. He had a way of preaching that kept people listening. He spoke simply, so that all could understand. He looked at his audience and talked as though he were speaking to each person alone. The people answered with "Amen" and "Hallelujah!"

He prepared his sermons well. He did not expect the Lord to fill his mouth with an "instant message." He studied and

44

prayerfully sought for new ideas, stories, or illustrations and for just the right words.

Carefully he would outline his sermon. Then he would let it "soak," going over and over it in his mind until he had it well memorized. Often he did this while lying in bed. No wonder God blessed his ministry so richly.

He would begin his message slowly, almost as if he were a little uneasy. But soon he would be in complete freedom. Sometimes he used bold motions with his hands to emphasize a point. His style was natural and pleasing. He was a master at keeping his audience attentive.

To close his messages, he used powerful sentences that would nearly lift the people out of their seats. Then the walls of the old tabernacle would ring with praises of joy.

This emotional excitement attracted people to the services. "Keep the glory down!" Dr. Bresee would say. He wanted God to be so near that the people would sense His presence and respond. Yet he constantly warned against extreme emotional display. Many who came to make fun of a service were so moved by God's Spirit that they stayed to pray.

Dr. Bresee rarely preached more than once on Sunday at the tabernacle. His assistant pastor or a guest minister would speak in the evening. He never went to the back of the church to shake hands with people as they left. Instead, he would stay at the front where those who had spiritual needs could come and talk with him and possibly kneel at the altar for prayer.

By the end of the first year, 350 members had joined the Church of the Nazarene. In five years the membership increased to almost 1,000. Calls began to come for Dr. Bresee to hold meetings in other cities and organize their groups as part of the Church of the Nazarene. God was showing Dr. Bresee that He had bigger plans ahead for him than just "The Glory Barn."

10

"Marching to Zion"

Clippety-clop, clippety-clop, went the horse's hoofs as Dr. Bresee drove his carriage home from Wednesday prayer meeting. With him were his daughter-in-law, Mrs. Paul Bresee, and several other members of the congregation. It was a pleasant summer evening in 1900.

Suddenly as they crossed some railway tracks, a speeding streetcar struck the carriage. The buggy was completely smashed. One of the women was killed instantly. All the others were injured.

Dr. Bresee was picked up unconscious and carried into a house nearby. His son, Paul, who was now a doctor, came quickly to care for his father and his own wife, and others of the injured.

It was several days before Dr. Bresee became aware of what had happened. It took him many weeks to recover enough to get out among people again. When he did appear in public, he looked and walked like an old man. A picture taken of him a short time later showed that his hair had turned white and his dark, full beard had been shaved off.

But there was still work for him to do. God had wonderfully spared his life and he did regain fair health. But for the rest of his life he was to feel the effects of the accident.

As soon as he could, he was back at the crowded tabernacle, preaching again. One morning an army colonel stood and asked if he might say a few words. Dr. Bresee consented. The man thanked the church for their prayers for his sick wife. Her recovery was so remarkable that he felt certain it was God's touch.

He said he wanted to show his thanks by a gift. He said he thought the time had come when the church should buy lots and begin building a permanent church. He handed Dr. Bresee $500 for that purpose. Immediately others responded and soon the amount was doubled.

A committee was appointed and property was purchased. Dr. Bresee began to plan ways to raise the $10,000 which would be needed to begin building. He thought of an idea. A $10.00 gold piece, a coin which was used in those days, was called a golden eagle. He would need 1,000 golden eagles. He described later how he presented the idea to the people:

> I told them that I would make my vest pocket an eagle's nest; that every ten dollars should be an eagle, every five dollars a wing, every dollar a quill, and every fraction of a dollar a feather, until the thousand eagles were gathered.

The people began bringing their gifts and soon there was enough to begin the new building. Dr. Bresee didn't want it to be fancy. He believed a church building should be plain and inviting to the poor. But the committee soon learned that there were city fire regulations to consider. They would have to build of brick, stone, and iron, not wood. This would cost almost twice as much. Some felt discouraged at first, but with prayer and faith they tackled the job. The money was raised and before long the church was completed.

On March 20, 1903, there was excitement around the old tabernacle. It was moving day for the Church of the Nazarene. The old building was already empty of its furniture. But it was packed with people, standing from wall to wall, and spilling out into the street.

With zest the audience sang. They probably used some of Dr. Bresee's favorites, such as: "Hallelujah, Amen," "Oh, Glory, Glory, Glory! Oh, Glory to the Lamb!" and "All for Jesus."

The assistant pastor led in an earnest prayer. He thanked God for the victories in the old tabernacle. It was here many had knelt at the altar and been converted and sanctified. Over and over again the glory of God had blessed the people. Here Dr. Bresee had baptized babies, married couples, and conducted funerals.

The old spike that had been driven into the wall when the building was begun was taken from its place and kept as a precious reminder of the church's early beginning.

There may have been some who felt a little sad to leave the old building. But these people were like their leader. They had a forward look. Whether it was morning or evening, Dr. Bresee always greeted people with, "Good morning." He insisted that it was always morning for the Christian, for his eyes are fixed on heaven.

The people that Friday night were anxious to be on their way to the new church. A procession formed at the altar, and poured out into the street. First were the torchbearers. They held their burning lights high to point the way. Then followed the musicians with instruments. There were cornets and drums. Next came the ministers, then the board members, and finally the people of the congregation.

Down the street they marched, shouting praises and singing

"We're Marching to Zion." Crowds joined the parade. It was thought that 10,000 people marched to the new church.

They crowded into the new building, which had seating space for about 2,500. Thousands remained in the streets outside, unable to enter.

Two days later, on Sunday, the building was dedicated. A prayer group met early that morning in the balcony. But before their prayer service ended, crowds had already begun to gather. Long before the service was scheduled to begin, the building was "filled to its utmost capacity."

Before Dr. Bresee could preach, a man feeling guilty for his sins came weeping to the altar. He asked for prayer that he might be saved. This did not disturb Dr. Bresee. It just seemed to emphasize his main purpose—the salvation of souls! For that, everything would wait.

After the man found peace in God's forgiving love, Dr. Bresee preached. He chose the prayer of Solomon when he dedicated the Temple in Jerusalem. "O Lord God of Israel . . . the heaven of heavens cannot contain thee; how much less this house which I have built!" (II Chronicles 6:17-18)

Then came the great dedication offering. The congregation marched up the aisles and past the row of tables placed over the altar. There they left their offerings. Ushers kept the people moving as quickly as possible, but the procession lasted 45 minutes and was more than a mile long.

After an offering prayer, the church board came forward. The chairman presented the building to the pastor. Then with great dignity Dr. Bresee dedicated the church to God. After prayer was offered, the high ceilings rang with the Doxology, "Praise God, from whom all blessings flow."

Over $10,000 was received in offerings that day. About 50 seekers prayed at the altar, and 20 new members joined the church.

The new building was large enough for great conventions, yet simple enough in style to make the poor feel at home. Besides the big auditorium, there were classrooms for a "complete" Sunday school.

The building also provided for the usual Sunday dinners to be served in the basement. Sometimes meals were being prepared while Dr. Bresee preached in the auditorium above. The meals were not served for money, but were freely given. Many a needy family, hungry for both physical food and the "bread of life," found a sense of belonging in that Christian fellowship Sunday noon.

Dr. Bresee had long been concerned about winning and using the children and the young people who came to his church. Even in the old tabernacle he had two young people's societies. By 1903 over 200 active young people were members of the Los Angeles church. The assistant pastor declared that those young people "ask no better entertainment than a good live prayer meeting. . . . A happier lot of young people cannot be found anywhere."

The annual Sunday school picnic was a high point of the year. A special train would be chartered and several hundred would go to Long Beach for the day. In 1904, over 1,000 went to Playa del Rey. After their relaxing at the beach, a big picnic dinner was served. Then the crowd gathered in a large tent for singing and preaching. Nearly every year seekers would find God before the day was over.

Dr. Bresee had a burning desire to lead men and women into the kingdom of God. He was a very wise and practical man. He was not afraid of difficult problems. God used him to bring great things to pass. He was leading these people as they went forward, "Marching to Zion."

11

Church with a Mission

The large, fashionable church downtown was proud of its name and reputation. Only people of high standing in the community belonged to it. But one day a shocking thing happened.

A regular service had begun. The dignified minister, in his flowing clergy robe, was leading the formal worship. Suddenly a good member stood and asked the pastor if he might say a few words. Everyone looked shocked. Whoever heard of anyone interrupting the ritual in this church? Had the faithful brother lost his senses?

Before the surprised pastor could object, the man began speaking. He told how he had been sanctified at a holiness meeting. He said the Holy Spirit had filled his life and cleansed out the sinful nature. He now had new power to live and witness for the Lord. As he spoke his face glowed with heavenly joy.

Some of the church members looked out of the corners of their eyes at each other. Their tightly set lips silently spoke their disapproval. They squirmed with embarrassment.

What effect would such a testimony have on their children? What would the visitors think? Those holiness meetings seemed to be affecting some of the best church members in town. Something must be done to quiet these people!

The church leaders decided to tell them never to testify to holiness again—at least not in church! If they continued, then they would be warned that their names could be dropped from the church roll. Other big churches had taken the same action.

But threats and ridicule did not hush the testimonies. The joyful Christians kept right on telling their friends that they had not only been forgiven of their sins and been converted, but they had found a further blessing. It was the abiding presence of the Holy Spirit in their lives. Many of their former church friends were no longer kind to them. They let them know that they were not welcome in their churches.

What should they do? They would certainly never give up their new experience and testimony. Should they try to stay in their old churches even though they were unwelcome? Or should they leave and join some independent holiness group?

Such were the problems of many Christians around the turn of the century, 1900. Hundreds of little groups of dedicated Christians across the country were gathering for Bible study and prayer. They would get together in some areas for holiness revivals, conventions, prayer bands, and camp meetings.

They came from many different churches. But they shared one experience. They had given their lives completely to God and had been sanctified by the Holy Spirit. They were called "holiness people."

If these small groups were to become stronger and stay healthy, they would need to work together. They would need some sort of rules for conducting their organization's business and would need some unified statement of their beliefs. This would mean they must have wise, practical leadership to bring this about. Already some misguided leaders were causing confusion among some of these sincere people.

Dr. Bresee began to realize the call of God to a special task. He saw the need for a national, even an international, holiness church, and he set out to build one. Growth came almost automatically. The Church of the Nazarene, which he had founded, was no longer a mission. But, as Dr. Bresee said, it was "a church with a mission."

As news of Dr. Bresee's work in Los Angeles spread, calls began coming to him to organize one group after another into the Church of the Nazarene. He began to urge true holiness people everywhere he went to join the Church of the Nazarene.

In 1898, delegates from these churches met together to prepare a handbook, or *Manual*, for the new church. It stated the beliefs and rules that Dr. Bresee had taught and practiced from the beginning in 1895.

He insisted that each congregation should have a say in choosing its pastor and be responsible for its own business affairs. Yet he felt there should be superintendents and boards, chosen by the people, to supervise the work. He was a very democratic leader. Over and over again, he urged the laymen to take the lead in starting projects and pushing them.

Dr. Bresee felt that the members of a holiness church must be united in what they believed was necessary to salvation. Yet they must show love and charity of spirit toward each other in lesser matters such as the way in which Christ would come again, or on how Christians should be baptized.

However, there were several odd ideas and teachings which Dr. Bresee just would not allow. He was careful not to take people into the Church of the Nazarene who had ideas that would hurt the church. Some, for instance, thought the church should have a strict set of rules on dress and behavior. Still others said that the Holy Spirit would cause one to speak strange languages that no one understood. Such strange talking was called "speaking in tongues." Then there were some who insisted that it was

53

sinful to take medicine when one was sick. They thought that one should pray for healing and never go to a doctor.

Dr. Bresee did not believe these things. He did not want the people who believed them to be members of his church, for it would cause confusion.

He was concerned that the church would keep the salvation of souls as its main business. He objected to members who urged the importance of other interests. "Our work," he declared, "is to preach holiness, to spread it over these lands. To this we give ourselves; for this we give our all."

Churches were organized on the west coast—in California, Washington, and Oregon. Then the movement began to leap across the nation. Dr. Bresee appointed an assistant to act as a sort of "advance scout." He was to visit interested groups and make plans for organizing them into the Church of the Nazarene.

In 1904, Dr. Bresee was called to Chicago to organize the Chicago First Church of the Nazarene. Other calls followed to Texas, Idaho, Utah, Nebraska, and Illinois.

One big help in spreading the church was its printed material. With the beginning of the Los Angeles tabernacle, Dr. Bresee started a small church paper. He called it the *Nazarene*, and used it to tell news about the church. By 1900 the paper was being published every week and was going to 32 states as well as several foreign countries. He urged his people to share their papers with friends and to get new people to subscribe.

Dr. Bresee saw the need for teaching and training holiness leaders. He was concerned that holiness workers be well prepared. But he was pressed by many other duties and could not push education as much as he wanted to at first.

A concerned group of women from different denominations in the Los Angeles area became burdened about the need of a Bible college. They formed a group to pray for the starting of such a school. They called themselves "The Bible College Prayer

Circle." As they prayed, they felt led to Dr. Bresee's group and joined his church.

They presented him with generous cash gifts and provided a building for a Bible school. Once again church members had taken the lead in pushing a project. In his paper Dr. Bresee wrote, "For some time this work has been pressed upon us; to open a school that would teach the Word."

In 1902, Dr. Bresee opened the school, which he called the "Nazarene University." He had a vision for a great university, not for just a small Bible school. He tried to lay a good foundation. (The school is now Pasadena College.)

Now in addition to being pastor of Los Angeles First Church, general superintendent of the Church of the Nazarene, and editor of the church paper, Dr. Bresee found himself president of this new baby college. At the age of 64, he was doing the work of three or four ordinary men. How long could he continue carrying such a load?

12

Birthday of a Denomination

Dr. Bresee brought his gavel down on the table. He was presiding over the first General Assembly of the Church of the Nazarene, being held in Chicago in 1907.

A group of churches from the northeastern United States who called themselves "The Association of Pentecostal Churches of America" were represented there. The two organizations had decided to join together to form a nationwide holiness denomination.

Of course, before such a union could be made, certain differences had to be settled. They quickly agreed upon their beliefs and their purposes. But the two groups had very different ideas about church government.

Some thought there should be district leaders to appoint all pastors and to supervise the affairs of each church. Others said that each congregation should be allowed to manage its own business. A church did not need higher guidance or authority.

The people from the East felt that churches should be independent. They should be joined to other holiness churches only in a loose sort of fellowship or association. Dr. Bresee felt quite strongly that there should be a central supervision if the organization were to succeed.

The assembly had to decide an important question: Was this new movement to be a denomination or just an association of churches?

After committee meetings, discussions, and much prayer, a plan was worked out that satisfied both sides. The united churches would form a denomination to be called "The Pentecostal Church of the Nazarene," using parts of both the original names of their groups. (Years later, the word "Pentecostal" was dropped and the denomination was once again called, "The Church of the Nazarene.")

There would be district and general superintendents and boards to oversee the work. They would help guide local churches in calling their pastors and in managing affairs of general interest. But the congregations would carry on their work locally as they wished.

When the vote for union was taken, everyone voted yes. "Amidst tears and laughter and shouts of holy joy," the resolutions were unanimously adopted. The union was completed.

These churches in the East had a Bible school and published a newspaper. They also had several missionaries in foreign lands. These too became part of the denomination. Now all across the northern part of the United States and reaching out into foreign countries, the new church was spreading.

At the assembly, a delegation of holiness people was present from Texas. They were called "The Holiness Church of Christ." Most of them were convinced that they too should join this growing denomination. However, there were some problems to be solved before such a union could take place.

The South had been deeply hurt by the Civil War. President

Lincoln had planned to rebuild the country with kind sympathy. But when he was assassinated, such plans perished. Some bitterness still existed between the South and the North. Feelings of mistrust entered even into religion. Some denominations had split over this, forming separate northern and southern branches.

Would it be possible, under such troubled conditions, for southern and northern holiness groups to join? What about the infilling of the Holy Spirit—this "perfect love" experience? Was it strong enough to overcome the mistrust and suspicious feeling between the states? Such a union would indeed take a miracle of holy love.

Besides these differences, many of the southern holiness churches held to very strict rules of dress and behavior. They felt that if they joined the Church of the Nazarene its *Manual* or rules would have to be enlarged to include this and some other matters. In fact there were four points they wanted to have added: (1) the way people dressed, (2) divine healing, (3) forbidding the use of tobacco, and (4) belonging to secret orders.

Committees were appointed to work out statements which would be acceptable to all.

Dr. Bresee thought the baptism of the Holy Spirit was a better guarantee of good behavior than strict church laws. But the Holiness Church of Christ in the South had for many years held to such rules.

Some said, Why bother trying to work out a compromise with the southern holiness people? If we cannot agree, let them go their way and we will go ours. But Dr. Bresee replied, "We cannot let them go; they are our folks." He had a vision of a great national church uniting all the holiness people across America.

In April, 1908, Dr. Bresee was called to hold meetings at the Texas Holiness University at Peniel, Tex. The Peniel community had members from many different denominations. For years they agreed simply to worship together in the college chapel without organizing a church. Often, however, they had felt the need for governing rules and for a regular pastor.

Dr. Bresee spoke in the college chapel. The time was right. He called for all those ready to unite with the Pentecostal Church of the Nazarene to meet him at the altar. One hundred three persons stepped forward. In a few moments a new church was organized.

The Holiness Church of Christ invited the Pentecostal Church of the Nazarene to hold its second General Assembly at Pilot Point, Tex. The idea was that perhaps a union of the two holiness groups could be worked out at that time. Thus in October, 1908, more than 1,000 holiness people from all over the nation met in a huge tent for this historic event.

The session began with a Communion service. God's nearness melted the people together in Christian love. As Dr. Bresee stated later, "From that time on nothing could prevent the union."

A compromise was presented to the assembly in which a balance was made between law and free choice. The chairman called for all those in favor of uniting into one church denomination to rise. Everyone stood.

The chairman announced a unanimous *yes* vote. At once God's blessing fell on the people.

A wiry little Texan jumped to his feet and started across the wide platform. "I haven't hugged a Yankee since before the Civil War," he shouted, "but I'm going to hug one now!"

At once, a large, 275-pound northern delegate with a long handlebar mustache leaped up from the other end of the platform. He met the Texan near the pulpit. Their "bear hug" was greeted by shouts and praises from the audience. People jumped to their feet waving handkerchiefs, clasping hands, and embracing others with whom they had differed.

The place could not contain their enthusiasm. A march

59

formed as the crowd sang, to the tune of "Dixie," a little chorus that was repeated across the nation.

> *With forces all united*
> *We'll win! We'll win!*
> *We'll preach a gospel o'er the land*
> *That fully saves from sin.*
> *Praise God! Praise God! Praise God*
> *For full salvation!*

The people marched out and around the great tent, finally forming an immense circle on the grounds. Dr. Bresee, nearing his seventieth birthday, climbed up on a chair. The sight of their founding leader, with his white hair, clean-shaven chin, and neat appearance, commanded attention.

With inspired words he addressed the multitude. The crowd applauded and shouted praises as he spoke. Every heart was moved. But probably no one was happier or more blessed than Dr. Bresee himself. He was seeing come to pass his dream of a great holiness church.

That day, October 13, 1908, became known as the official birthday of the Church of the Nazarene.

13

The White Rose

"Dr. Bresee doesn't look very well, does he?"

"No, he doesn't. I wonder how much longer he can carry on." The whispered words passed among the delegates attending the Third General Assembly, held in 1911.

Everyone had begun to notice that their leader's health was failing. He accepted his reelection as one of the three general superintendents. But he had already begun to give up other work. With a little sadness, he had resigned that year as pastor of Los Angeles First Church. Someone else became responsible for the Nazarene University. And yet another was chosen as editor of the church paper.

Being a very humble man, he did not realize his greatness. He did not see the sacrifice he had made across the years. His wife and family had been a wonderful help to him.

In his later years, the grown sons happily paid most of their father's personal bills. This freed him to make his daily rounds, calling. Mrs. Bresee usually went too, seated beside him in their buggy. All over the city of Los Angeles he would drive their old white horse. Faithfully he called on the people, emptying his pockets as he visited the poor and needy.

He loved and respected his wife. Whenever he mentioned her in public he always called her "Mrs. Bresee," and never any pet name. He let people know how much he appreciated the way she carefully supervised his clothing and travel bags. She saw to it that he had every needed item while away from home on his many trips.

As his health slowly became poorer, Mrs. Bresee traveled beside him. She was a delightful companion. Her loving care helped him with the strain of his work.

From state to state he traveled, conducting district assemblies and helping plan for the good of the churches. His heart condition made it impossible for him to bear much physical effort. Yet he was able to put amazing energy into his sermons. He preached almost every day and as much as three times a day.

He had rare ability as a leader. But his outstanding trait was his spirit of kindness. Old age did not make him bitter in any way. Instead, he became more long-suffering toward others. He would not say or believe anything evil about his fellow workers.

He still enjoyed life. He could see the funny side of things and laugh long and loud at a good, clean joke. He loved people and welcomed any who came to see him. Even though he was busy, he always had time to listen to the problems of others and to help in any way he could.

It was no doubt his close prayer life with God that kept his spirit so gentle. He would arise early every morning to talk with the Lord.

In 1915, Dr. and Mrs. Bresee spent the month of August at the summer home of one of their children. It was on a beautiful island off the coast of southern California. They had thought the rest and change of climate would help Dr. Bresee. Instead, he became seriously ill and was rushed home.

He slowly recovered but was never strong again. He constantly had trouble breathing. He found it difficult to sleep and lost his appetite.

In spite of his doctor's concern, Dr. Bresee insisted upon going to the General Assembly that fall. It was to meet in Kansas City, Mo. He had all his preparations made early. This included the procedure for business and the writing of the long report of the general superintendents.

This assembly, he felt, was of special importance. There were problems of leadership to be settled. Also, two other groups of churches were to unite with the Church of the Nazarene. One group was from Tennessee, called the Pentecostal Mission. The other was from the British Isles, the Pentecostal Church of Scotland.

In September, he bravely boarded the train headed for Kansas City. With him were his wife, their daughter, and their daughter-in-law, Mrs. Paul Bresee. They were all delegates to the assembly.

On the way, Dr. Bresee's breathing grew much worse. Most of the Southern California delegates were in the same coach. They became very concerned and held a prayer meeting there on the train. His condition improved.

As soon as they arrived in Kansas City, Mrs. Paul Bresee sent a telegram for her husband to come to Kansas City. He was a skilled doctor, and was able to help his father to keep going.

Dr. Bresee was well enough to take part in the opening business session. He was able to read the long superintendents' report, which lasted 45 minutes. When he finished, the assembly stood. They clapped their hands and praised God.

That same afternoon he gathered enough strength to conduct the Communion service. He was very feeble. Yet in his old-time way, he preached a wonderful message. He used his favorite scripture, the fifty-third chapter of Isaiah. The Word of God touched every heart. It was a wonderful service.

The following Friday, Dr. Bresee was reelected a general superintendent. After the election, a group came marching down the aisle and presented him with a huge bouquet of roses. There were 77 roses, a rose for each year of his life. But one rose was white. They explained that the white rose stood for the present year, which was not yet finished.

With Mrs. Bresee standing beside him, he responded to the gift of love. He expressed his thanks and assured the crowd that he would try to be around until the next General Assembly. But, should he not make it, he would wait for them at the "Eastern Gate over there."

That white rose was very appropriate. Dr. Bresee never completed that year.

14

The Eastern Gate

With the close of the General Assembly of 1915, it looked as if Dr. Bresee's work would soon be done. The trip home to Los Angeles was very painful. Never again would he be able to preach, or conduct a business meeting. He knew the days for him were very few. But he was content. He had done what he could.

All during his pastorate at the old Los Angeles tabernacle and at the new building Dr. Bresee would be at the door to greet people as they came to church. With a sincere word and handshake, he welcomed every boy and girl, man and woman who came.

"But, Dr. Bresee," a visiting misister objected, "isn't this getting to be too much for you? The church crowd is so large now. Some mornings there are as many as 1,000 people. Shaking hands with all of them takes so much of your energy. You still must go to the pulpit to preach. Why do you keep doing this?"

With a smile Dr. Bresee explained. "I count it one of the richest privileges to stand and take them by the hand as they come!" Then he added, "I often pray that I may be permitted to

welcome all of them at the Eastern Gate of the New Jerusalem."
He meant, of course, that he hoped to meet them in heaven.

One Sunday a feeble, old lady, with trembling steps, approached the church. Gently Dr. Bresee helped her enter. "Oh, thank you, Pastor," she said, squeezing his hand. "I do hope you'll be at heaven's gate to help me when I get there."

Dr. Bresee laughed and reminded her that when she got to heaven she would not need his assistance. "But," he assured her, "I'll meet you just inside the Eastern Gate."

A minister friend, I. G. Martin, heard those words and set them to music. He called the gospel song "The Eastern Gate," and dedicated it to Dr. Bresee.

I will meet you in the morning,
  Just inside the Eastern Gate.
Then be ready, faithful pilgrim,
  Lest with you it be too late.

I will meet you, I will meet you,
  Just inside the Eastern Gate over there.
I will meet you, I will meet you,
  I will meet you in the morning over there.

On Thursday evening, November 4, 1915, Dr. Bresee called his family together. As his wife and loved ones knelt around him, he prayed for each one. He thanked the Lord for the love and kindness of his children and asked the Saviour to bring them all to heaven.

Two nights later an old friend came to see him. They talked of the problems and victories in Dr. Bresee's 60 years of preaching. Before the friend left, Dr. Bresee said there was one thing he wanted him to remember. "Position is nothing," he said; "reputation, little. True godliness is the only thing which has any value."

During those long and weary days of suffering, he spoke

only words of kindness. At times his strength improved so that he could talk to small groups who came to him.

One evening some of the leaders of the church and the university came to see him. He sat on the edge of his bed, with a quilt wrapped about him. The night was chilly, but the windows were open so he might breathe more easily.

In a voice that trembled with both age and tenderness, he gave them his parting words. He urged them to forgive everyone who had ever hurt them. He begged them to humbly live and work together in the love of the Holy Spirit.

He faced death without fear. In fact, he joyfully looked forward to it. He knew that his Lord was waiting for him. In his usual able way, he took care of all the family and church business that he could. He was ready.

"Never waste time," he had said many times. "It is too precious." Always Dr. Bresee had been punctual. He never had wanted his services to begin late. Certainly, he would be on time for this last appointment.

On November 13, 1915, Dr. Bresee quietly left this life to meet his Saviour, "just inside the Eastern Gate."

Three days later his funeral was held at his beloved church in Los Angeles. It was not a sad time. Long before the set hour of two o'clock, the sanctuary was crowded and hundreds began to gather outside.

The flower-draped casket was placed in front of the altar that day at 10 a.m. During those few hours between then and the funeral 2,000 men, women, and children walked past it. He was loved by his people.

The pastor of the church opened the service with prayer. He told the people that Dr. Bresee had conducted more than 2,500 funerals during his ministry. Always he had tried to make God's loving presence seem real to those who came.

At Dr. Bresee's own funeral, God's presence seemed very near. The text for the funeral sermon was Psalms 37:37: "Mark the perfect man, and behold the upright: for the end of that man is peace." The words seemed very fitting for a man who had preached and lived perfect love.

As his casket was carried to the Evergreen Cemetery, a great procession of horse-drawn buggies, carriages, chartered streetcars, and a few early-model automobiles followed.

His body was laid to rest in the midst of the things he loved so well: waving grass, stately trees, sweet-smelling flowers, and singing birds. Five years later his beloved Maria was buried beside him.

Over his grave is a modest monument. It bears the simple words:

BRESEE

Rev. P. F. Bresee

1838 1915

Founder of the Church of the Nazarene

*   *   *

Back in 1895, Dr. Bresee began the work of the Church of the Nazarene. He had only 100 or so faithful supporters to start with. During the 20 years that followed, he led that church to become a denomination of nearly 32,000 members. It extended over the North American continent and across to the British Isles. It had 800 local churches, a publishing house, several colleges, and scores of missionaries in foreign countries.

Many years have passed since Dr. Bresee's death. Thousands have gone to meet him "inside the Eastern Gate." But still his influence lives on.

The church he organized, and for which he gave his last bit of strength, continues. Today the Church of the Nazarene has grown to over a half million members.

The teaching of holiness is still its central doctrine.

His basic plans and methods for church management which he first worked out are little changed today. They are found in the *Manual* of the Church of the Nazarene.

His concern for the needy and minority groups has not died. The Church of the Nazarene has a growing outreach to all classes and races of people around the world.

His interest in publications which began with his early church paper, the *Nazarene Messenger,* has been continued. Today the Nazarene Publishing House produces and mails tons of church-printed matter every day. Its books, audiovisual helps, and Sunday school supplies go to its almost 7,000 churches, and the official church paper, the *Herald of Holiness,* goes to 200,000 subscribers.

Dr. Bresee's interest in the youth of the church is still seen. Active programs are planned for children, teens, and young adults in fellowship and soul winning.

His love for music continues to characterize the church. The Lillenas Publishing Company is one of the largest publishers of gospel music in the world.

Dr. Bresee's concern for education has influenced both the ministry and the laity of the Church of the Nazarene. Today, in addition to a seminary for graduate study, the denomination has many colleges, Bible schools, and day schools in America and abroad.

This godly man wanted everyone to know of the saving and sanctifying power of Jesus Christ. He felt that every Christian should experience the power of the Holy Spirit in his life. He knew it could keep one free from sin and help him grow more like Christ.

With his rather off-tune voice, he would join the people in singing, "There is power, power, wonder-working power." Loudly he would sing out that word "power" and clap his hands to emphasize it. For he knew of God's power. It had cleansed out his sinful nature. It had given him strength to live a victorious Christian life.

Through the years, he went about preaching the words of Jesus: "Ye shall receive power, after that the Holy Ghost is come upon you" (Acts 1:8). That was the power that helped Dr. Bresee to organize the Church of the Nazarene. That was the power that brought him all the way to "the Eastern Gate." That power still lives in the organization he founded—the Church of the Nazarene.

Bibliography

Anonymous, by A Fellow Servant of the Master. *Holiness in Doctrine and Experience.* Kansas City: Beacon Hill Press, 1951.

Bresee, P. F. *The Certainties of Faith,* Ten Sermons by the Founder of the Church of the Nazarene, with an introduction and notes on the author's life by Timothy L. Smith, Ph.D. Kansas City: Nazarene Publishing House, 1958.

Bresee, Dr. P. F. *Sermons on Isaiah.* Kansas City: Nazarene Publishing House, 1926. (Compiled by C. J. Kinne, Foreword by J. B. Chapman.)

Brickley, Donald P. *Man of the Morning.* Kansas City: Nazarene Publishing House, 1960.

Corbett, C. T. *Our Pioneer Nazarene.* Kansas City: Nazarene Publishing House, 1958.

Girvin, E. A. *Phineas F. Bresee: A Prince in Israel.* Kansas City: Nazarene Publishing House, 1962.

Hills, A. M. *Phineas F. Bresee, D.D., A Life Sketch.* Kansas City: Nazarene Publishing House, n.d.

Manual, Church of the Nazarene. Kansas City: Nazarene Publishing House, 1968.

Martin, I. G. *Dr. P. F. Bresee and the Church He Founded.* Kansas City: Nazarene Publishing House, 1937.

Ramquist, Grace. *The Boy Who Wanted to Preach.* Kansas City: Nazarene Publishing House, n.d.

Smith, Timothy L. *Called unto Holiness.* Kansas City: Nazarene Publishing House, 1962.